SOME HEART SOME MIND

DIKSHA NARANG

Dear Mommy, You are the best And out of all of them You always choose me And make me laugh With your pretty cool jest;

Thank you for being you And for never making me feel aloof; I will be by your side Because this world is not so safe And not worthy of your faith.

Contents

Preface *vii*

Acknowledgements *ix*

About The Author *xi*

1. My Guardian Angel 1
2. We Need You, Krishna 3
3. Blessed With The Best 5
4. Thank You God 6
5. My Backbone 7
6. Let It Be Now 8
7. Dear Dad 9
8. My Dear Mom & Dad 10
9. Oh Life! Why So Strife!? 11
10. Dear God 12
11. Let's Unite Now 13
12. I Will Never Hate You 14
13. My Forever Friends 15
14. True Love 16
15. Never Leaving You Alone 18
16. Future Talks 19
17. Those Days With Them 21
18. My Guru 22
19. Marriage, Not Adjustment 23
20. God, Oh God... 25
21. My Favourite God 26

Contents

22. She Is The Best 27
23. My Faith In You 28
24. Nothing Without You 29
25. Let's See What Awaits Us 30
26. We Are There For You! 31
27. My Parents 32
28. Why!? 33
29. Patriarchy: No Equality 34
30. Says A Woman In A Patriarchal Society 35
31. A Change 37
32. My Extended Family 38
33. Utopia 39
34. Their Ill-fate 41
35. Chapter 35 42
36. A Dynamic Journey 43
37. Letting It Go 44
38. My Guiding Force 45
39. Anything For You 46
40. Dear Friends 47

Preface

This book is a compilation of open letters and poems wherein the author reflects on her life while addressing some of her known ones that includes her family and friends. The author has also tried to pen down her feelings about connection with God. Some of the pieces of work are written on social issues too that have become important to address. Author considers this as her duty to address these issues to bring about a change in society and as they say pen is no less than a sword, so author has tried to convey message through her writings.

Acknowledgements

Firstly, I would like to thank Poetic Souls Publication for organizing 40 days writing challenge and providing budding authors like me a chance to fulfill their dream of getting their book published easily Fulfilling my dreams would never have been possible without my family's support, especially my mother. She has always encouraged me to write and read, and here I am today, being recognized as an author. Heartfelt thanks to my family. Last but not the least, I would like to thank my family like friends, who have been a constant support to me and motivated me to give my best in everything.

About The Author

A new poet and writer in this world full of writers, Diksha Narang. She feels that writing your heart out is the best way of relieving your mind and making you feel better. She believes that she is still a new author who has been writing for one year now. She aspires to be a teacher, but she also wishes to write a novel once in her life. She concerns her writing with social issues, but majorly she uses writing as a medium to express her thoughts and feelings. Some social issues she has written on are problems faced by women, new generation, and increasing inhumanity in the world. Her works also reflect on her deep connection with God.

CHAPTER ONE

My Guardian Angel

Dear God,

I believe in your existence around me, and your every child. I can sense your presence around me. You have helped me many a times during tough phases of my life. There are days when I feel helpless because of which my mind doubts on your existence, but even then, my heart believes that you are there watching on me and making ways for me to solve my problems on my own.

I know that you are aware of all my happiness and sadness. I am sure that you are my guardian angel guiding me towards good, and protecting me from evil. So much so far, I have realized that through these problems you are putting me on tests so that I come out of them to become a strong-minded and high-spirited woman. Maybe you have big plans for me because I have too, for myself.

I believe in you. I trust you for all that you do for me. I have faith in you. I know you might be busy, but that you still guide me, and make me feel your presence, it makes me happy. I know that even before me saying anything you get to know of it. That's why sometimes you fulfill my wishes without even me asking for it. Please be with me, always. Please be my guardian angel, forever.

From,
One of your child

CHAPTER TWO

We Need You, Krishna

Dear Lord Krishna,

I have heard stories of your mischievousness since I was a child. I learned from childhood that you killed your own uncle for he was wrong and unrighteous ruler and even inhumane. When I grew up more, I started to understand your role in Mahabharata war, in the life of Pandavas and in the life of Draupadi. When Draupadi was insulted in front of all men and her dignity was at stake, you helped her, even when you were not there. You were a great son, great brother and great friend. You helped everyone, no matter if they were known to you or your strangers.

You helped Draupadi, and gave example of what happens when a woman is insulted in any way. But people are not taking that example seriously or maybe to them, that was not a lesson when Kauravas were killed for their heinous act. It is maybe because they are not punished now. Punishment is far away a thing as some of them are not even scolded for that, rather they are protected from being punished by law. Was it for Draupadi only? Now can't we women expect to get justice from you or from law?

I have grown up hearing your stories, and I still believe in your powers. Please don't ever let my trust break. I will fight if something like this happens to me, but can't you take re-birth once again? Can't you once again set an example for modern Kauravas? I hope that you will. I will wait for it because I trust you.

From,
Your devotee

CHAPTER THREE

Blessed With The Best

Dear God,

I am forever grateful to you, God for everything you have provided me with. You have given me with more than I could ever wish for. I feel blessed for whatever you have granted me and for whatever you have in store for me. But there's one person in my life who you have blessed me with and I am extremely thankful for that. And that person is my mother. No words or nothing can express my gratitude for her presence in my life. I am the luckiest child on this earth to have a mother like her. She is my everything.
Thank you, God, for blessing me with such a supportive and loving mother.

CHAPTER FOUR

Thank You God

Dear God,

No matter how much I have struggled in past few years, but my faith is still headstrong towards you. Whenever I felt lost, I knew you were the one I need to seek for in my heart. And it is with your blessings that from last year my life has changed to a great extent. Even I have changed and I know whatever I am today is path you have guided me to. It would never have been easier without your guidance and blessings. Though years before last year was a difficult time but you made it a little easier and now just perfect for everything you have blessed me with. Please keep guiding me towards good whenever I feel lost on my path.

CHAPTER FIVE

My Backbone

Dear Mummy,

You know you are my everything. I can't even think of my life without your presence in it. Don't ever think that I need you for you do almost all of my work even till now. I might be dependent on you for my work but that doesn't mean I need you only for that. I need you because you are my backbone. I need you because you understand me more than anyone in my life. And I love you because whenever you scold me, just after a few minutes you love me even more. I love you because I got this life by you. I love you because you are always there for me, supporting me throughout. Thank you for making life even better by just your presence.
I Love You Mommy

CHAPTER SIX

Let It Be Now

Dear God,

No matter how much I try my best in relations, they still misunderstand my intentions. No matter how much I try to be calmer, they still think I am a rude person. I don't doubt myself, but I don't think I can take it anymore. I have tried my best, somewhat for those relations I have with them and somewhat for my own good, but my efforts always go unnoticed. I don't think I will try anymore. I don't think it affects me anymore of what they think about me or my behavior.

CHAPTER SEVEN

Dear Dad

Dear Papa,

You are a great dad in almost all aspects. But I still feel a gap in our relationship. I don't know if it's generation gap that others also feel, or is it the difference of opinions, or is it your ego, or is it my ego. I don't know what it is. But I want that gap to be bridged. I want our all mis-understandings to be solved as soon as possible. I know you think that my mom is my only best friend and that I care for her only, but I care for you both and I love you both. I want you too as my best friend. I want that understanding between us too. I really hope this day comes soon.
I Love You Papa

CHAPTER EIGHT

My Dear Mom & Dad

Dear Mummy Papa,

I know you both love me a lot. You are best parents when it comes to fulfilling my demands, loving me and taking care of me. But there is something more important that I want you do for not just me but for you both too. I want you both to focus on your relationship. I know there are fights in every relationship, but what I don't like is end number of misunderstandings between you both. And it hurts me when I see you guys arguing almost all the time, and then you don't even clear out your misunderstandings. Can you just please at least try to understand each other. You have to live your whole life with each other so why not live happily like soulmates. I hope you can do this for me.

CHAPTER NINE

Oh life! Why so strife!?

Dear Life,

Some days you have been nice while some days you were not so kind towards me. You have taught me various lessons and things have been pretty fine till now. But sometimes you just do too much in spite of what I expect out of you considering my behaviour towards everyone. Why are you always rough to those people who are good towards everyone and never seem to trouble anyone? I understand that you do this to make me courageous and valiant. But please be a little nice. I hope you understand that some days it gets too much and then it becomes difficult to handle situations you throw at me. Please be kind.

CHAPTER TEN

Dear God

Dear God,

You do so much for entire universe. You have created earth and all of us are your child. But sometimes I feel like you have given men more privilege. I don't know whether I should even say this, but there are times when I doubt your planning for earth and people residing in it. You seem not-so concerned about women. I know that you are not wholly responsible but they have learnt it from you only that the men are superior. Can't you make it all right? I know I also need to do something for this, but without your support I can't. So, can you help me?

CHAPTER ELEVEN

Let's Unite Now

Dear Society,

You are always making norms and deciding behaviors on the basis of gender, but why it seems to me that these behaviors affect the life of women more! Don't you people also feel the same at times? I have felt this many a times because I am also one of the victims of it. It is because of your biases that I cannot talk to a boy freely and that I cannot wear dresses of my own choice. It is because of the internalized patriarchal thinking of you people that I am considered weaker and inferior than men. Don't you also think that you are too partial towards just men, and I know that most of you are taught this from your ancestors, but it can be changed too, right? So, why don't we unite and bring a change for the betterment of all of us?
I really hope that you will give a thought to it. And if you will do so, then I am sure that this will be considered our contribution in the development of our country.

CHAPTER TWELVE

I Will Never Hate You

Dear Younger Self,

You were immature and impulsive, but now people call me rude. I don't think I am rude. I just believe that I have become opiniated in a positive sense that is good for myself and more straightforward which makes me more confident. And I don't blame you for my straightforward self. I would rather like to thank you for being a way of bringing change in myself. I have learned from you to be mature and take life more seriously. I don't regret being you because it is through you that I have learned few really important lessons of my life. It is because of you that I am now leading a happier life. I will not remember you with sadness of doing certain mistakes, rather I will always remember you as the learning self of my life. Thank you for being a part of my transformation in becoming a sensible being.

CHAPTER THIRTEEN

My Forever Friends

Dear Books,

With you, I have a bond that I share with no other on this earth. People tell me not to believe in you, but I still do because I know that even if my hopes won't come true but, in that moment, I get ecstatic and my worries disappear. I believe in fairytales because of you and it is because of you that I am learning to be happy in my own utopian world. Things around doesn't bother me when I have you to spend time with. Through you I have experienced roller coaster of emotions and learned to control those overwhelming emotions. I don't think that I will ever share this kind of bond with anyone or anything.

CHAPTER FOURTEEN

True Love

Dear Dimple,

I still get numb when I think of you and your love story. None of us can feel what all you have grown through, but at least we can learn a bit from you. You are a perfect example of true love, which nowadays cannot be found easily. Nowadays people can't even wait for days and you waited for him to return and even when he came back wrapped in tricolor, your love didn't die with him, rather you are living a life with his memories and love. You could have married and no one would have blamed you, but you chose to live with his memories and this is what makes your love story eternal.

Nowadays girls and boys promise each other many things, but when it comes to bad phase of life, they don't withstand each other. I don't believe in this kind of love. Even though people would have appreciated and praised your story, but they still won't understand and apply it in their lives. Our young generation is such that they don't understand the true meaning of love. And when it comes to truly understanding each other and being there for each other, just like you and Vikram Batra did, even the word "love" seems small to describe it. I feel grateful to have known your story and I really respect your

decision.
Thank you for sharing your story with us and letting us all know what true love means.

CHAPTER FIFTEEN

Never Leaving You Alone

Dear Brother,

First of all, let me remind you a most important thing that I love you a lot. And I know that you too love me and maybe even more than I do. You don't express it through words but your actions explain it all. I have seen you caring for me. And sometimes even fighting for me from mom and dad. I still remember those good old days when we both bonded so well. We never needed anyone else to play, share things, talk and also fight. Let me tell you that you are still dear to me and I really miss those days.

Our parents might not understand what you are going through right now, but I do. I want you to know that you have me, now and will have me always when no one will be there to talk to you or understand you. I know you are going through a rough phase of life, but don't worry everything will be fine.
Love you bhai!

CHAPTER SIXTEEN

Future Talks

To,
My Older Self,

I really don't know what the future has in store for me. I cannot change things if they are predestined, but as it is said that God decides our future based on our actions, so we can always take care of that. I have always tried my best not to do things that are unethical or not morally right, or that my intuition doesn't permit me to do. But to not take any chance I would like to advise you a few things.
I have always tried to never do wrong to anyone and would like to continue trying the same my entire life, and I want you to know that when we do wrong to someone, we can never be happy so always remember this thing. Next is being honest. Sometimes, most of us lie to someone close to us or any known ones, and if you are lying for good and not for any misdeed, then it's fine, but if you are lying for something unlawful, or immoral, then you are not on the right path. So, please be considerate of this fact and be honest to everyone and most importantly to yourself. Last and another important thing I would like to advise you is that beware of fake people and fake friendships. You will meet many people who will be an expert in pretending or faking things. Always be cautious of this.

Know who are your well-wishers and who are back-bitchers. Never trust anyone easily, but don't be too hard on yourself and others while befriending someone.
I hope that the best things await our future, and so all the best to us!

CHAPTER SEVENTEEN

Those Days With Them

Dear Cousins,

I hope you guys are doing fine. Today I saw a group of cousins on Instagram, and they were all happy and enjoying together, and that reminded of our past times. Do you also remember those gleeful days? I remember them very clearly because those were the days when we were together, and everything was just fantastic. We were close enough and that's why we never felt need of any such friends to share and enjoy, but things have changed now. We don't share things with each other anymore and things are quite distant between us.

We don't share same bond now, but I still want things to get better between us all. Even though now we have friends, but that doesn't mean we cannot have a bond like those childhood days again. I have tried at times to build that bond again but didn't feel the same reciprocation from your side. No worries, and I want you to know that I still want things to become good. So, if you also feel the same, we can surely work on it. And I don't know if you guys miss those days, but I really do.

CHAPTER EIGHTEEN

My Guru

To
My Favorite Teacher,

In India, we have worshipped teachers as "Guru" from the ancient time. They are even given the status of Gods in our country. I was taught the same by my parents to give teachers respect. And I never felt that I should respect them because my parents said so because almost every teacher I got was so polite, caring, and lovable towards me. But there is one teacher whom I will always remember as my favorite teacher. She is such a humble person and a kind one too. She supported me and understood me in my hard times, and not only this but she also advised me with the best.

These days students don't give that much respect to their teachers. It is understandable that now things are franker between teachers and students, and thus it's like a friendship between them, but sometimes students become disrespectful in some situations. And this is not the right thing. Teachers-students can become friends, but that respect should remain in that friendship.
I feel grateful to have friends like teachers and would like to thank them for being a mentor and guide to me.

CHAPTER NINETEEN

Marriage, Not Adjustment

To,
My Would-be Husband,

My dear would-be husband, today I want to say something to you. I don't know when or how we will be meeting, and I won't lie to you that I will try to be an ideal wife because no one is perfect, and that's a fact. I won't even want you to be a perfect man because there will be times when we both might make some mistakes that might affect our relationship. I will give my best to make things as they were, but only if you, too, want things to be better. And I hope you will understand that it's not my duty only to make our marriage successful because we will be partners, so that becomes the duty of both of us and not just me.

I will expect some things and you will also, but we will not burden each other with our over-expectations. I won't say that I will do all household chores with my job because I won't. We both will handle all the things together, and I want you to know it beforehand. Also, I don't know if you will need your personal space or not, but I won't be too nosy. And I expect the same from you. And obviously, I will be loyal towards you and our marriage and will expect the same from you because that is extremely important in any relationship.

These are not some guidelines or anything like that, but just my definition of marriage. And everything that I have mentioned is not something out of the box because this is basic in a relationship like husband-wife, where we have to spend our lives together. And when these things are in place, I guess everything will become perfect.

CHAPTER TWENTY

God, Oh God...

Oh God
For them,
You are the almighty
You are the ultimate power
But for me,
You are a guardian angel
And you are my protector.
They believe
You reside in temples and mosques
But I believe
You live in our hearts.

CHAPTER TWENTY-ONE

My Favourite God

From birth
You were a naughty child
But loved by every kind.
Your stories
World-famous they are
For they portray your glories
To everyone
Near and far.
You came on earth
And made it worth
By teaching people a lesson
A lesson of never living in oppression
And to fight against repression.

CHAPTER TWENTY-TWO

She is the Best

Her hands make the most delicious dishes
Her mind can solve my problems
Her heart that beats for her loved ones
Is full of love for me and everyone in the family
And her blessings that are always with me
Protect me from evil and every negativity.

CHAPTER TWENTY-THREE

My Faith In You

A difficult time it was
But just like always
I believed in your powers
And you made it easier
And healed my scars.
Tough times come and go
But you have been there.
Always
To help me go through and grow.
I hope you will always stay
And will never betray.

CHAPTER TWENTY-FOUR

Nothing Without You

Mom,
Without you my life is incomplete.
You have taught me
To be a kind person
To never accept defeat
And to be my best version.
Please be with me forever
Because I don't want to lose you
Never ever.

CHAPTER TWENTY-FIVE

Let's See What Awaits Us

If you still don't understand me
If you still don't understand my intentions
Then I don't think
That you are one of my loved ones.
I have tried my best
To make you understand
Of my stand
But you always protest
No matter whatever I said.
And now I can't do it anymore
Because now it irritates me to the core
So, lets leave it now on God.

CHAPTER TWENTY-SIX

We are there for you!

You are the best dad
You make me glad
But I see you are sad.
You make sure
That we get everything
That we want
But you even leave those things
That you are interested in
And that too many a times.
We understand everything
And so,
You don't have to sacrifice from now
Because now it's our turn
To learn and return.

CHAPTER TWENTY-SEVEN

My Parents

An arranged couple
Not at all alike
With contrasting beliefs
And different lifestyles.

Partners they are, but
Their conflicts are endless
However, as parents,
They are the best.

Full of goodness
And truly selfless
Forms of purest love
And kindest in the world.

CHAPTER TWENTY-EIGHT

Why!?

Why can't you be nice?
Even when I have been wise
And you do this every time
As if I have committed a crime!

Why only good people?
You try to make feeble
And those doing things illegal
You don't do much wrong
To those people.

CHAPTER TWENTY-NINE

Patriarchy: No Equality

I don't understand this God
If this your plan
To make men
Superior in every clan
Or is this the society
That has made men
A deity
To be worshipped by women
And thus, making patriarchy
In society, more prevalent
And in making women subservient.

CHAPTER THIRTY

Says a Woman in a Patriarchal Society

Why do you have to do this?
Time and again
You have just blamed me
Always.
Is it because I am a woman?
That you just summon me
And not those
Who have made these baseless rules,
To make women's life terrible.
Is talking to men a wrong thing?
Because they call me names when I do this
Oh please now don't act as if you're shocked
As you are one of those
Who have made the norms,
Oh, the 'biased' norms
For men don't have to worry
Even when they rape someone
While a woman is treated badly
Even when she makes a mistake
Of just adding a little more salt
Or even when it is just the doubt of men in her family

That she is having an affair.
In all this
You have also played a part
And ruined everything
What could have been a bliss.

CHAPTER THIRTY-ONE

A Change

She was a fool
But was cool
She was happy
She was laughing
But things have changed now...

She is happy
But laughs no more
Like she used to before
They think that she ignores
But what they don't know is
That she just doesn't say anymore
No matter how much it hurts her
Because she knows
That they don't care for her.

CHAPTER THIRTY-TWO

My Extended Family

Sometimes you may be far away
But never from my heart
You guys are leaving.
Without you
I may still be alive
But the fun that is there because of you
Will no more be there without you.
I may not say all the time
But always remember
That you are the rhyme
To the poem of my life.

CHAPTER THIRTY-THREE

Utopia

There is a world
A little far
A world
Of positive vibes
Where truth prevails
And not like this world
Where evil stays,
And betrays
What can I say of that?
Because it's now the part
Of everyone's lives,
But that world
Is not like this
There,
Love wins over hate
And there are people
With whom I can relate
Because in this world
People are two-faced
And have always façade
That I have never liked.
So, I would love to go there
Where I don't have to be beware

And no one stares
No matter what I wear.

CHAPTER THIRTY-FOUR

Their ill-fate

Your story
A love-story
That not just I
But many admire.
Yours was a true love
But your ill-fate
You had to part ways
But you never left him
And now
Living with his memories
From that day
When he left you in this way,
When he left the world
And you were alone
But you stayed strong
And decided to be alive
For him
For your love.

CHAPTER THIRTY-FIVE

You always bother
But no one can take your place
My dear brother;
You in trouble
And your life a tussle
Make things in our life muddle;
How do I make you understand?
That you are taking wrong stands
But even after that
We always withstand
And will never misunderstand
But now you need to know
Of the high time
And let people know
That the show must go on.

CHAPTER THIRTY-SIX

A Dynamic Journey

There were times
When nothing made sense to me
And everything was chaotic
Thus, people seemed to me idiotic.
Such was the phase
That seemed to me, a maze.
But then it came
Like a shooting star
That fulfilled all my wishes
And made me realize
The true meaning of my existence
Things were coming back to track
And I was learning to not just defend
But also, to attack
So that I don't have to depend
On people who always pretend.
My life, which was once a barren land
Was now becoming a fruitful land
And fruits that it bore
Were sweeter than before
But it was all possible
When I learned to explore
And became more responsible.

CHAPTER THIRTY-SEVEN

Letting It Go

Like a cat
You have spent your life
I think it was my mistake
To trust someone like you
Who was not even worthy of a chat;
Though I still want to befriend you
But let me tell you
This time
I won't let you fool me
For I have discovered all your fabricated lies
That destroyed happiness in my life
So now let bygones be bygones
And let's move on in our lives.

CHAPTER THIRTY-EIGHT

My Guiding Force

You supported
Whenever I needed.
You told me ways
Of getting success in life
And not lies,
I know it
For I worked on those ways
To reach my destination.
I still remember
That once you told me
To try and try
Until you don't learn
How to fly;
And I will always be grateful
For you have made me learn
To fly high
In the skies.

CHAPTER THIRTY-NINE

Anything for you

You don't need to be perfect
And I will still respect
Because I know
You will always do your best;
You will be my best friend
And know
That there will be no end
Of my love
And that I will never intend
To hurt you in any sense;
But, if someday I did
I will mend it all
With my love
That is all for you
And just you.

CHAPTER FORTY

Dear Friends

You are all precious to me. You all make me happy and life makes more sense when you are with me. Sometimes I hurt you but it is never intentionally because I never want to lose you. I might be rude at times but it is because with those loved ones we don't have to pretend anything and that's why I always say whatever I feel. I have always wanted to give my best in making this friendship last forever. And I know you guys wish the same that's why we have come this long. There have been endless arguments, but it has only made our bond stronger. So, cheers to our forever friendship

Printed by Libri Plureos GmbH in Hamburg,
Germany